D1484825

SONG OF COURAGE

SONG OF FREEDOM

The story of the child,
Mary Campbell,
held captive in Ohio by the
Delaware Indians from 1759-1764

by
Marilyn Seguin

BRANDEN BOOKS
Boston

© Copyright 1993
By Branden Publishing Company

Library of Congress Cataloging-in-Publication Data
   Song of courage, song of freedom : the story of the child,
Mary Campbell, held captive in Ohio by the Delaware Indians from
1759-1764 / by Marilyn Seguin.
      p. cm.
   Includes bibliographical references and index.
   Summary: Details the kidnapping, captivity, and return of an
Ohio girl by Delaware Indians in the eighteenth century.
   ISBN 0-8283-1952-9
   1. Campbell, Mary, fl. 1764--Juvenile literature.
   2. Delaware Indians--Captivities--Juvenile literature.
   3. Ohio--Biography--Juvenile literature. [1. Campbell, Mary,
fl. 1764.   2. Delaware Indians--Captivities.   3. Indians of North
America--Captivities.]
      I. Title.
   E99.D2S38 1993   92-44001
   977.1'01'092--dc20   CIP
   [B]   AC

Entire text was produced with *Pages & Windows*
for WordPerfect 5.1 (DOS)

Branden Books
Division of Branden Publishing Company Inc.
17 Station Street
Box 843 Brookline Village
Boston, MA 02147

Dedication

To my committee: Ellen and Don, Jodi and Ed, Kathy and John, who provided lots of support and encouragement as I worked on this project. Thanks also to my husband Rollie and to my children Scott and Katy. This book was their idea in the first place, and their interest spurred me on.

Acknowledgments

My interest in the history of the Indians who once inhabited my home town was inspired by Virginia Bloetscher's book, *Indians of the Cuyahoga Valley and Vicinity*. I am also indebted to Virginia for assisting me in tracking down many of the illustrations for my book. In fact, the Edith Steinkraus drawing of the women and children working in the cornfield appears in Virginia's book, and she gave me permission to include it here.

Two other books were especially useful in my research. John Heckewelder's *History, Manners, and Customs of the Indian Nations Who Once Inhabited Pennsylvania and the Neighboring States* was a gold mine of information and anecdotes about the Delaware Indians. I am also indebted to the late Big White Owl, author of *Big White Owl Relates Traditions of the Delaware Indians*. The legend of lost opportunity is among the many beautiful stories and legends in his book.

I am grateful to the staff of Taylor Memorial Library in Cuyahoga Falls, as well as to the Cuyahoga Falls Historical Society for their assistance and cooperation in making available the historical documents I needed to complete the research for this book. Finally, I'd like to thank my friend and fellow writer, Jane Turzillo, who read early versions of the manuscript and made suggestions for improvement. Jane also traveled with me to several of the sites described in the book, and her photographs are included in these pages.

TABLE OF CONTENTS

Prologue

In the fall of 1764, the Ohio Indians turned over 206 white captives to COL (Colonel) Bouquet at his headquarters on the Tuscarawas River. The surrender of prisoners was a condition of a treaty signed earlier that year. Among the white captives was a young girl, Mary Campbell, returned by Chief Netawatwees of the Lenni Lenape Indians (Delawares). COL Bouquet witnessed the parting of Netawatwees and the girl, and he later wrote that it was a tearful and touching scene. In fact, he noted that many of the returned captives were reluctant to return to their white families and some had to be tied up to keep them from escaping.

This is the story of Mary Campbell's kidnapping and captivity. Because Mary apparently left no written record of her years with the Indians, we can only guess at what her life must have been like. And while most of the events and people in my story are real, other details will remain forever shrouded in mystery.

This Benjamin West drawing depicts the return of the captives by the Indians in 1764. British Cololel Henry Bouquet is seated at the right. Many of the captives developed close ties with their captors and were reluctant to return to their white families. (Drawing courtesy of the Library of Congress).

Chapter 1

On the Banks of the Susquehanna

Mary Campbell hummed softly as she helped her mother pack the picnic basket. Carefully, she wrapped a clean napkin around the johnny cake Ma had just taken from the oven. The thick corn bread smelled delicious and Mary popped a few crumbs into her mouth. She sneaked a peek to see if her mother was watching--Mary didn't want Ma to think she was taking something that she could not have. After all, they had baked the johnny cake for their neighbors. But Ma hadn't seen her. She was busy putting a lid on a jar of fresh honey that would also go into the basket.

Ma was so kind and thoughtful. She was always concerned about others who didn't have it as easy as did the Campbell family in their snug little cabin on the bank of the Susquehanna River. The Campbell family consisted of 10-year-old Mary, her brother Dougal and Ma and Pa.

"Mary, sweet," said Ma, "I'm going to take this basket of treats over to Mrs. Liggett this forenoon. Mrs. Liggett has been feeling poorly since the wee one was born. I think this basket will cheer her up. You keep an eye on young Sammy when he wakes, so's Mrs. Stewart can do her chores."

Mary looked over at the trundle bed set in one corner of the cabin. Young Sammy Stewart was asleep under one of Ma's own patchwork quilts.

Sammy was the son of Mr. and Mrs. Stewart, who were staying with the Campbells while the Stewarts cleared the land for a cabin of their own. The Stewarts had planned to sleep in their wagon while they set up their homestead, but Ma had insisted that Mrs. Stewart and young Sammy sleep inside the Campbell cabin.

"We've plenty of room, Abby, " Ma had told Mrs. Stewart. "And I do think your young 'un is sniffling. A child with a cold shouldn't be sleepin' in a damp wagon."

In the end, Mrs. Stewart and Sammy agreed to sleep in the cabin, though Mr. Stewart bunked down in the barn every evening after the two families shared their supper.

If the nice spring weather held out, the Stewart cabin should be ready in a few weeks, Pa told them at breakfast this morning. Pa, Mr. Stewart and Mary's 14-year-old brother, Dougal, were already at the clearing, working on the cabin. They worked on the Stewart building part of every morning, but most of the afternoon time they spent preparing the fields for planting so that they would have enough food to eat all through the long, cold Pennsylvania winter.

Ma was tying her bonnet, getting ready to run her errand. Mary thought her mother was beautiful. The red calico bonnet framed her mother's oval face. Wisps of Ma's curly brown hair fell across her forehead. Why, Ma looked just like a young girl, Mary thought, and she smiled up at her mother.

"When I get back, Mary, perhaps we can make some fresh ginger tea to take to the men. Looks like it's going to be a fine, warm spring day. The men'll be thirsty at their work," said Ma.

"Oh, yes, Ma, let's," said Mary. "And then let's walk by the river and find some fiddleheads for our supper." Mary was excited about the idea of getting away from the cabin for a while this afternoon. Ma and Pa did not allow her to go too far away from the cabin lately. Pa said there had been reports of Indians in the area. Ma and Pa were afraid of Indians. Mary could tell from the frightened look in Ma's eyes whenever Pa spoke about them, which wasn't often. Ma shushed Pa and Dougal whenever they started to talk about Indians if Mary was within earshot.

Ma bent over and gave Mary a kiss. Ma smelled so good and fresh, just like the lavender and cedar wood that lined her clothes trunk. "I love you Mary. Look out for Sammy when he wakes. His Ma'll be back from the barn with fresh milk shortly. Then you children can have johnny cake and fresh milk for your lunch."

"Bye, Ma," said Mary, and she closed the door behind her mother, pulling in the latchstring as she had been taught, even though the day was warm and bright and she longed to keep the door open. Maybe she couldn't keep the door open--Mary would never go against what Ma and Pa told her to do--but she could at least open the window to let in some of the warm, fresh breeze. Mary glanced at little Sammy. He was still asleep. She would have to step on his bed in order to reach the window because the bed was pushed up against the wall. If he woke up, she'd really have her hands full.

Sammy whined a lot because he was always sick. He'd been sniffling since the Stewarts joined them more than six weeks ago. Sometimes Sammy's fussing woke everyone up in the middle of the night.

Then Mary had a hard time getting back to sleep, and she felt cranky all the next day. Mary didn't like to get cranky, because then Ma would become annoyed with her.

Mary carefully stepped up onto Sammy's mattress. Her weight made the bed shift, and Sammy stirred. But now Mary could see out the window. Pa had made the window out of glass the Campbell family had brought with them in the wagon when they moved from Connecticut. Ma and Pa were proud to have a glass window, instead of the oiled paper windows that most of their neighbors had.

Through the thick, wavy glass, Mary could see the barn, where Mrs. Stewart was milking the two cows. Since the Stewarts joined them, Mrs. Stewart had taken over the barn chores because Mrs. Stewart said she ought to earn her keep. Mrs. Stewart was grateful that she and Sammy could sleep inside the Campbell home where it was warm and dry. Before the Stewarts came, it was Mary's job to go to the barn to gather the eggs and Dougal's job to milk the two cows. Mary missed going to the barn in the early mornings with her brother.

Mary took a deep breath and raised the window a crack. She put her face to the opening and gulped in the fresh air. The air smelled moist and fresh. Mary rested her head on her hands and looked through the window opening. Beyond the path that her mother had taken to the Liggett cabin was a dense forest. Mary thought she saw something move just at the forest's edge. Probably a deer, she thought. The Pennsylvania woods was full of game and often the animals would come into the path and the clearing where the cabin sat. Mary shifted her weight and stood on tip toes on the soft mattress to get a better look.

At her feet, Sammy stirred and whimpered. Mary looked down at him. Sammy was two years old. Mary knew she ought to feel sorry for the little fellow, being so sick and miserable all the time, but mostly, Sammy just annoyed her. Now he was looking up at her, his face all twisted up, getting ready to cry. Didn't the child ever wake up happy, she wondered.

Mary stepped off the mattress and lifted the boy up. "Now, now, Sammy, sweet," she said, "don't cry; it's a beautiful day. Your Ma went to the barn to get us some good milk. And there's honey to put on our johnny cake. Don't cry now, Sammy," crooned Mary.

Sammy looked at her for a moment, and then began to wail loudly. Mary found a clean handkerchief to wipe his nose, and she began to sing softly a tune that Ma had sung to her every night when she and Dougal were small. Soon, the little boy was soothed and he quieted some. Mary held the boy cradled against her, humming the sweet tune, wishing he'd go back to sleep. It wasn't time for him to wake up from his nap yet. If she hadn't stepped all over his bed, he'd probably still be sleeping, she thought. She continued to hum, and soon Sammy's eyelids grew heavy as he drifted back into sleep. Quiet, peace and quiet. She could almost take a nap herself.

Then Mary heard something outside the cabin that made her spine tingle and gave her gooseflesh all over. She heard the high-pitched whoops of angry men. Still holding the sleeping Sammy, Mary stood up and looked out the window. Indians! Quickly she dumped the sleeping boy into her mother's clothes chest and closed the lid.

Chapter 2

The Capture

The wild whooping sounds were coming from the direction of the barn. Smoke drifted in through the open window. Oh no! The barn is on fire, thought Mary wildly. Mrs. Stewart was in the barn! And so were the two milk cows, Sarah and Bossy, and the chickens, and Pa's most prized possession--their plow! How would they ever manage without their plow!

Mingled with the wild whoops of the Indians, Mary now heard the piercing shrieks of Mrs. Stewart. Quickly, Mary scooted herself under Ma and Pa's bed. She shut her eyes in terror. Those Indians had come from the direction of the path her mother had taken just an hour before. What if they had killed her Ma, beautiful, kind Ma? Again, Mrs. Stewart screamed, and this time her cry was closer. From the barn, Mary heard the pitiful sounds of the family's milk cows, bellowing in fear of the fire. Then Mary heard the sound of a hatchet burying itself in the door of the cabin.

From her hiding place underneath the bed, Mary could see moccasined feet moving through the cabin. There must be ten Indians in the cabin, she thought. She heard the sound of Ma's dishes breaking as they hit the floor. The Indians continued their loud whooping, and Mary thought she could also hear the muffled cries of Sammy who was hiding in the trunk. Then Sammy's cries grew louder. The Indians must have opened the trunk and found him. Sammy's screams grew louder, more desperate. The Indians were hurting little Sammy. She had to help him. Mary crawled out from under the bed.

Before she could get to her feet, a big Indian grabbed her by the arm and hauled her out of the cabin. Outside, the air was filled with smoke from the burning barn, but through the haze Mary saw Mrs. Stewart. An Indian was holding Mrs. Stewart's arms pinned to her sides, but her head was thrashing back and forth as she tried to get away from him. Inside the cabin, she could still hear the terrified cries of Sammy.

Pa and Dougal and Mr. Stewart will see the smoke and they will help us, thought Mary. But please, God, let Ma be safe. Mrs. Stewart, her pretty blue dress torn and dirty, was crying for Sammy, watching the cabin door. Soon, two Indians came out of the cabin, carrying Ma's pillowcases stuffed with things from her home. One of the Indians dragged Sammy, still crying, from the cabin. When Mrs. Stewart saw him, she fell forward in relief and her cries stopped.

The big Indian who held Mary shoved her forward in the direction of the river. The Indian dragging Sammy gave him to Mrs. Stewart, who clutched her son tightly, as she, too, was prodded in the direction of the river. Before they left the clearing, Mary glanced back at her home. The barn was totally in flames now, and Mary thought she saw a thin column of smoke rising from the roof of the cabin as well. The Indian behind her shoved her forward. Whenever her steps slowed to a walk, the Indian behind her would push her forward roughly, urging her to hurry, hurry. If they were in such a hurry, thought Mary, surely their rescuers must be close behind.

To keep from falling, Mary concentrated on the footpath. This is the very path Ma took this morning, Mary thought. Did the Indians come this way? Did they come across Ma? Or were they right now headed toward the Liggett home where Ma was? Mary tried to think of a way to warn Ma and the Liggetts if they got close to the cabin. But before they reached the Liggett home, the Indians and their captives left the well-worn foot path and entered the dense forest.

The Indians capture Mary Campbell and the Stewarts. (Illustration by Judy Botz Newhall).

Chapter 3

Scalped!

The Indians seemed very much in a hurry to get away. Mrs. Stewart said that was because the Indians knew they were being followed and that soon they would be rescued. They hurried through the forest and at night they slept on the hard ground. Sammy cried a lot. Mary felt like crying too, but she knew it would be babyish and it might make the Indians angry. Mrs. Stewart made Mary and Sammy say their prayers every night.

After five days of traveling, no one came to their rescue. Mary was afraid. Each day she was moving farther and farther away from Ma and Pa and her bother Dougal. Mrs. Stewart tried to make her feel better. "Don't worry, Mary. The men must have seen the smoke from the burning cabin. Even now Mr. Stewart and your father must be on our trail. Surely we'll be rescued at any moment," Mrs. Stewart said. But Mrs. Stewart was worried too--Sammy had a runny nose and a fever, and he cried most of the time he was awake.

One evening when they stopped to sleep, two Indians disappeared into the woods and didn't return that night. But when they returned at dawn the next day, they were carrying a fresh scalp. One of the Indians was wounded and he died later in the morning. The Indians carried the body with them along the trail until they came to the place where a great tree had fallen. The Indians removed the bark from the dead tree and carefully wrapped it around the body of the dead warrior. Then they moved aside the great tree trunk and placed the bark-wrapped body inside the earth's depression. They replaced the log over the grave and arranged the leaves and branches around the area until it looked as though the log had never been disturbed, except that it was missing its bark. Mrs. Stewart said that was so that the body could not be discovered by their rescuers, but Mary didn't think so. She thought it was an Indian funeral.

After that, the Indians moved their prisoners even faster along the trail. Whenever her steps slowed, the Indian behind Mary beat her ankles with a branch, urging her to hurry, hurry. Sammy's cold was worse now, and he had to be carried along the trail. Mrs. Stewart and Mary took turns carrying him, but they were weak from lack of food and sleep. After a while, one of the Indians hoisted the boy on his back, and for two days the Indian carried him through the forest. Then, one evening, the Indian carrying Sammy dropped behind the others. When he reappeared, he was alone. On his belt hung a bloody scrap of flesh that Mary recognized as Sammy's scalp.

When Mrs. Stewart saw her son's scalp, she rushed at the Indian, shrieking, "I'll kill you for this, you devil's heathen! And you'll burn in hell for eternity!"

That night Mrs. Stewart told Mary to memorize the trail so that they could escape. "But Mrs. Stewart, if we try to get away, the Indians will do to us what they did to poor Sammy. Maybe we should wait for Pa and Mr. Stewart to find us. They'll have guns, and they will bring others to rescue us, maybe even the army from Fort Pitt," said Mary. But Mrs. Stewart said that Mary should memorize the trail "just in case."

Mary hurried along. She was tired and cold from sleeping too many nights on the damp earth. She was trying hard to keep up. Once, when she stumbled on the path, the Indian behind her beat the backs of her legs with a leather thong, urging her to hurry. Today she sensed some new excitement among the Indians. Perhaps their rescuers were close by and the Indians knew it.

Most of all she was hungry. All she'd had to eat since her capture was dry cornmeal washed down with a bit of water she drank from her cupped hands. The Indians, too, only ate the cornmeal, she noticed, sharing it equally among themselves and their captives. Strangely, it made Mary feel full, even if it didn't taste very good. But they must have eaten up their supply, because there had been nothing to eat for the last day.

Suddenly, the Indian, who was the leader of the raiding party, raised the scalp pole and let out a loud whoop, and then three more cries in rapid succession. Ahead of her, Mary could see thin wisps of smoke rising above the tree tops. With a sinking feeling, Mary realized they were nearing the Indian village. Now they would never be rescued, she thought, for how could a few white men dare to take on an entire Indian village.

Again, the Indian in the lead let out four loud whoops and quickened the pace as he led the captives into the clearing of the Indian village. Behind them, the other braves were whooping and hollering, and one of the Indians pushed Mary and Mrs. Stewart into the clearing. They had reached the Indian village at last.   Indians rushed at them from all directions now. Terrified, Mary and Mrs. Stewart watched as the Indians of the village--men, women and children-- formed two lines, creating a tunnel to the center of the village. The Indians held branches and sticks ready to strike them, and they screamed at the terrified prison- ers, urging them to enter the tunnel. This was the dreaded gauntlet Mary had heard Dougal talking about. Prisoners must "run the gauntlet" he had told her, without falling, until they reached the safety of the pole at the other end. If one of them should fall, she would most certainly be beaten to death by the excited Indians.

Mary grasped Mrs. Stewart's hand, and the two prisoners ran past the shrieking Indians, who struck them on their shoulders and backs with their sticks. Finally, at the end of the line, Mary and Mrs. Stewart fell to the earth in front of an upright post set into the ground, and painted red. At first Mary thought the post was covered with blood. Soon it will be covered with my blood, she thought. On every side of them were Indian men, women and children, shouting, laughing, and tugging at their clothing and their hair.

Mary squeezed her eyes shut and prayed that her life would be spared. "Please, dear God," she prayed, "let me live to see my Ma and Pa and Dougal. Give me strength, and give my family the strength to find me." Next to Mary, Mrs. Stewart loudly cursed her tormentors and spat in the faces of the Indian women, who were fingering her hair and her clothes. In her agony, she dared the Indians to kill her.

Just when Mary thought she could not stand the commotion another minute, the Indian leader stepped to the painted post and raised the scalp pole.

The village fell silent. Putting her arms around Mrs. Stewart, Mary shut her eyes, shaking with fear.

Chapter 4

Song of Courage

"They are going to kill us now, Mrs. Stewart. I will never see my mother and father or Dougal again. They will never know what became of me. I am so afraid," sobbed Mary, as she hugged Mrs. Stewart tightly. A sharp "Shhh" from Mrs. Stewart warned her that she was talking too loudly.

"Better to die than to live amongst these heathens, Mary. I embrace death--in heaven I'll be with my baby Sammy. Be brave now, sweet Mary. Don't give these savages the pleasure of knowing you are afraid," whispered Mrs. Stewart.

The Indian leader spoke to the village for several minutes and then he was silent. When he had finished, Mary saw a young Indian girl and two Indian women, one with an infant strapped to her back, approach the painted post. The Indian leader lifted Mary to her feet, even as Mrs. Stewart tried to hold her back, and pushed Mary towards the woman with the baby. Mary was too weak with hunger and fear to resist. The woman with the baby and the young Indian girl led her to a wigwam near the center of the village. The wigwam was built of poles stuck into the earth and bent over into a domed shape. The whole structure was covered with bark and animal skins.

Mary noticed that all of the dwellings in the village were built the same way.

The Indian girl lifted the deerskin that was the door of the dwelling, and let Mary inside, where Mary sank to the floor in exhaustion. Outside the wigwam, she could hear the angry shrieks of Mrs. Stewart. And then suddenly there was silence--and Mary wondered if Mrs. Stewart got her wish after all.

That night, Mary slept on soft deerskins next to the young Indian girl. She dreamed that she was back with her family in the cabin on the Susquehanna. In her dream, she heard Sammy crying and she went to him and sang him a cradlesong to soothe him to sleep. And then Mary dreamed no more that night.

The next day at dawn, the entire Indian village packed up their belongings and, with their reluctant captives, began a long journey to the west. Mary despaired of ever seeing her family again. A few times on the long journey, Mary talked to Mrs. Stewart, who always reminded her to act as her mother taught her. Mrs. Stewart also told her to memorize the trail so that when the time was right, they could escape. But Mary thought she could never remember--there were too many pathways, and they had traveled too far and for too many days.

The Indian girl called Little Squirrel, whose sleeping furs Mary shared at night, stayed with Mary all the time. Mary was glad of her companionship, and she liked helping Little Squirrel take care of the girl's infant brother, Rain Boy.

Rain Boy was a remarkable baby, cheerful and easy going. Mary and Little Squirrel took turns carrying Rain Boy in his cradleboard along the trail during the day. The cradleboard was made of wood, cut into a flat oval shape, rubbed smooth so there would be no splinters to harm the baby or the carrier. Mary liked to tie the soft leather straps that held Rain Boy securely to the board. More leather straps fastened the cradleboard to Mary's waist and shoulders. Rain Boy gurgled and cooed happily whenever Mary bounced along the rocky trail with the baby on her back, and when the trail was flat, she would some-times skip every other step just to make Rain Boy giggle.

As they walked side by side, Little Squirrel spoke to Mary in the Lenni Lenape language and Mary tried hard to learn the words so she could speak to these Indians. But the language was so difficult--not easy like the English she spoke. Mary learned that *lenno* meant *man*, but *wuskilenno* meant *young man*, and Rain Boy was a *pilawetit*, a *boy baby*. The language was confusing at first, but Mary learned quickly and Little Squirrel was a patient teacher. Over and over, Little Squirrel repeated the words, pointing to different objects along the trail. One morning as they walked, Mary stepped on an *achgook*, a *snake*, and later that evening they ate *maschilameek*, a *fine trout* that Little Squirrel's father speared in the stream.

Mary learned words for ideas as well. She learned that *wulik* meant good, but *wulaha* meant better. A fine morning was *wulapan*. *Machkeu* was red, the color of the sky as the sun set; and *kschie-chek* was clean, like Mary's hair when she and Little Squirrel bathed in the river early in the morning. Soon, Mary spoke in short Lenape sentences. But Mrs. Stewart became very angry when she heard Mary speak the Indian words. So Mary was careful not to talk to the Indians if Mrs. Stewart were nearby.

In the Indian language, Little Squirrel helped Mary to understand that she had been presented by Little Squirrel's father, Chief Netawatwees, to his wife, Quiet Doe, to make up for the death of their girl child named Red Leaf. Mrs. Stewart had been presented to Quiet Doe's sister as a gift because her husband had been killed during the Susquehanna raid. Mary wondered if that dead Indian was the one whose forest funeral she had watched with Mrs. Stewart and Sammy.

It was spring time, and the trees were budding. The days and nights grew warmer as they travelled. Mary's dress, the blue one her mother made for her, was soiled and torn from her travels. Her shoes had long ago worn out, and Quiet Doe had given her a pair of soft deerskin moccasins to cover her feet. She longed for a short tunic like the one Little Squirrel wore. Mary's long dress was hot and the skirt caught at her legs when she had to climb the steep trail.

Sometimes on the journey, the Indians made-camp for several days and hunting parties were sent for meat. The women gathered firewood. The children, including Mary and Little Squirrel, foraged for berries and other edible plants. Little Squirrel showed Mary what could be eaten and what could not. When everyone returned to camp, the Indian women made a stew of whatever was at hand--berries, nuts, leaves, and when the hunting party returned, fresh meat. All the food was shared equally, but the men and boys were served before the women and girls. At first, Mary shared Little Squirrel's wooden bowl and spoon, waiting until Little Squirrel ate until she filled the bowl for her own meal. But one day while they were camped, Little Squirrel showed Mary how to carve out her own bowl and spoon. After that, Mary and Little Squirrel ate at the same time, and Mary was glad that she didn't have to wait for her food anymore.

Sometimes, when they couldn't make camp along the trail, they all ate *pemmican,* a mixture of dried meat, berries, nuts, and animal fat, which they packed into pouches and carried with them. And there was always the cornmeal mixture that Mary had first eaten when she and Mrs. Stewart and Sammy were captured. This mixture was eaten in small amounts, with water. Little Squirrel told her it was dangerous to eat more than two palms full at a time because it expanded inside the belly.

They left behind the mighty mountains of Pennsylvania and entered the country the Indians called the *Oyo*, or Ohio, following a well worn trail long used by the Indians. One day, they left the trail, and followed instead a river the Indians called the Cuyahoga. The river wound its way through a deep gorge, with sandstone cliffs rising steeply from the river's banks. Soon they came to a bend in the river which emptied into a shallow, but wide waterfall. On the north side of the river were caves for shelter and woods for hunting. On the south side of the river were flat fields, suitable for planting. Little Squirrel's father, Chief Netawatwees, leader of the Turtle Tribe, decided that this would be the permanent camp.

That first night in their new camp, Mary and Little Squirrel, along with the other Indian women and children, slept in the shelter of a shallow, wide cave. Mary and Little Squirrel spread their sleeping furs in the soft sand on the floor of the cave and fell asleep listening to the water rushing over the falls below them. Between them, Rain Boy wriggled in delight.

His belly was full and he was clean from his bath in the river.

The night was warm, and the air was fragrant with vegetation coming to life after the long winter. It was such a beautiful spot, and Mary thought she could almost be happy here. Back home, Ma sometimes let Mary and Dougal sleep outside, under the stars, on warm nights like this one. Ma, oh Ma, I miss you so much thought Mary. Please find me, I want to be with you. But Mary knew that she was a long way from her home in Pennsylvania. She had traveled so long, she had come so far, how would Pa and Dougal ever find her now? Tears swelled in her eyes and spilled down her cheeks. She was glad that Little Squirrel was turned away from her and couldn't see what a baby she was.

Beside her, Rain Boy sighed softly and stirred in his sleep. Mary put her lips to Rain Boy's ear and hummed him Sammy's favorite cradlesong.

In 1759, Mary Campbell was adopted into the family of the Delaware Chief Netawatwees. This drawing by Arnold E. Boedeker is a study sketch for the painting shown on the cover of this book. (Used with permission of Cuyahoga Falls Historical Society.)

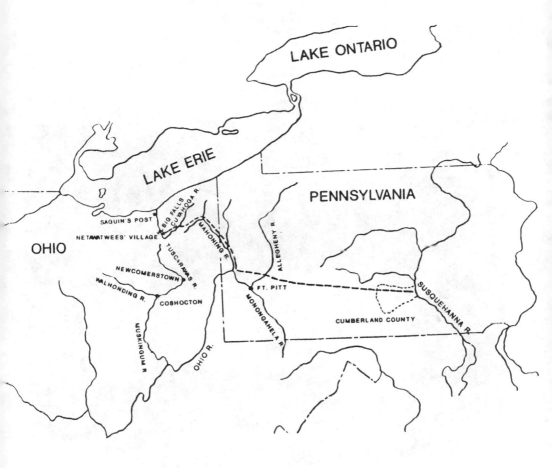

LAKE ONTARIO

LAKE ERIE

PENNSYLVANIA

OHIO

SAGUIN'S POST

BIG FALLS

CUYAHOGA R.

NETAWATWEES' VILLAGE

MAHONING R.

TUSCARAWAS R.

ALLEGHENY R.

NEWCOMERSTOWN

WALHONDING R.

COSHOCTON

FT. PITT

MONONGAHELA R.

SUSQUEHANNA R.

CUMBERLAND COUNTY

MUSKINGUM R.

OHIO R.

– – – – – MARY'S ROUTE FROM PENNSYLVANIA TO OHIO

This map shows the trail over which Mary Campbell and the Indians may have traveled as they migrated from Pennsylvania to Ohio. Mary Campbell is thought to have been the first non-Indian child to come to this part of Ohio. (Map by Roland Seguin.)

The Big Falls of the Cuyahoga River, near the cave where Mary Campbell stayed with her Indian family. (Used with permission of Taylor Memorial Library.)

Mary Campbell with her Delaware Indian family. Painting by
Arnold E. Boedeker. (Used with permission of the Cuyahoga
Falls Historical Society.)

Chapter 5

She-who-sings-sad-songs

The seasons passed, and Mary grew accustomed to the ways of the Indians whose wigwam she shared in the village above the falls of the Cuyahoga. Mary reckoned the passing of time, like the Indians, in seasons rather than in years. The seasons were divided into moons rather than months.

August was the moon of roasting ears, because the ears of corn were then ready to be eaten. October was the harvest moon; December the hunting moon. Mary's favorite moon was March, the sap running month, because at that time, the sap ran from the maple trees. During the sap running moon, the Indians traveled to the maple groves to gather the liquid from the trees and turn it into sugar.

First, they cut little openings into the bark of the maple trees and fitted wooden taps into them. The sap flowed out of the taps into suspended containers. When the containers were filled, the children gathered the sap and poured it into one large container in which it would boil until the liquid evaporated, leaving the good thick maple syrup that would sweeten their meals for most of the coming year.

The winter moons were especially hard, and sometimes there was not enough to eat. When the snows were deep, the men might leave for days, in search of game. In the meantime, the Indians of the village would eat whatever stored provisions they had, but they often ran out of food before spring. One time, Quiet Doe had to kill their pet dog for food to sustain the family until Netawatwees and the other braves returned from a hunt.

When the ground thawed and the dogwood leaves were the size of squirrels' feet, it was time for the women to plant corn. Planting and tending the corn took up most of her time, but she enjoyed the work. It made her feel useful. Whenever she was working in the fields, Mary's thoughts flowed through her like a song. Sometimes, to the delight of the others working beside her, Mary would sing her songs out loud in her contentment. But everyone noted a tone of sadness on her face and in her voice.

As she worked, Mary sang the words to the slow and soothing cradlesongs taught to her by her mother. That is how Mary earned her Indian name, She-who-sings-sad-songs. And from then on, except when she was in the presence of Mrs. Stewart, who insisted on calling her Mary Campbell, Mary became known as She-who-sings-sad-songs.

Little Squirrel was her constant companion. Little Squirrel taught She-who-sings-sad-songs how to plant corn the Indian way. First they loosened the soil with spades made from the shoulder blades of elk fastened with sinew to handles. But a few of the Indian women used metal spades like her father used in Pennsylvania. The Indians traded furs for these spades and their tools with the French trader, Saguin, who lived down-river. With sticks, the women then made holes in the ground and dropped three kernels of corn into each hole, covering them with crushed shells from the river. They planted beans in the side

of each corn hill. As they grew, the bean plants would
be supported by the cornstalks.

To discourage weeds, the women planted
pumpkin squash amongst the beans and corn. Little
Squirrel said that corn, beans, and squash were
inseparable, and she called them "the three sisters."

She-who-sings-sad-songs grew healthy and
strong as she worked and played in the Indian village,
and for the most part, she was happy. She-who-
sings-sad-songs and Little Squirrel were now both
twelve summers old. Only two thoughts disturbed
Mary's contentment. Sometimes at night, as she lay
beside Little Squirrel in the wigwam, She-who-sings-
sad-songs thought about her mother and father and
her brother Dougal in Pennsylvania. She missed
them. She hoped that they were safe and that they
did not worry too much about her. Very often, She-
who-sings-sad-songs would cry herself to sleep,
thinking about her family and her old life in the cabin
in Pennsylvania. But in the morning, she was always
bright and cheerful and glad to be working beside her
sister Little Squirrel.

The second problem that troubled She-who-
sings-sad-songs was the way Mrs. Stewart treated her
whenever they chanced to work beside each other in
the cornfield. Mrs. Stewart had grown more angry and
bitter during her captivity. The Indians called her
Angry Woman. She lived in the wigwam of Quiet
Doe's sister, Seagull. Seagull was always prodding
Mrs. Stewart to work, and angry voices were often
heard from the wigwam of Seagull. Clearly, Mrs.
Stewart was not happy.

Whenever Mrs. Stewart was near She-who-
sings-sad-songs, she scolded her for her friendship

with Little Squirrel. One rainy day, Quiet Doe sent She-who-sings-sad-songs to deliver a message to Seagull. When She-who-sings-sad-songs entered the dwelling, Mrs. Stewart was there alone, sewing moccasins. "Mary, please come in. I have something to say to you, child," Mrs. Stewart scowled. Mary sat cross legged beside the woman. "I saw you yesterday, working in the cornfield beside that heathen child you follow around like a puppy. What I saw chilled my blood, child. I saw you remove your tunic and work bare chested just like these savages. It is sinful, Mary, sinful! You must not adopt the ways of these savages. You must remember you are white, and preserve your dignity."

She-who-sings-sad-songs was ashamed at Mrs. Stewart's scolding. It had been hot working in the cornfield that day. She had outgrown her blue dress soon after her captivity, and Little Squirrel had helped She-who-sings-sad-songs to make new clothes from the soft skins of animals. She-who-sings-sad-songs's favorite tunic was made of the skin of a deer that her father Netawatwees brought back from a hunt. Little Squirrel and Quiet Doe showed She-who-sings-sad-songs how to scrape the skin clean with the rib bone of an elk, working the skin until it was soft and pliable. Next, the skin was tanned over a smoking fire before being cut and sewn into a tunic. Quiet Doe had decorated the garment with beads from the trader Saguin and with porcupine quills she dyed in a kettle over their cook fire. No squaw in the village had a prettier tunic than she, thought She-who-sings-sad-songs.

But because they lived in the forest, the Indians did not encumber themselves with unnecessary clothing. When it was hot, the Indian women often removed their tunics and worked only in their wrap-around skirts. She-who-sings-sad-songs had not been bashful to remove her own tunic on the day Mrs. Stewart saw her. "I am sorry if I offended you, Mrs. Stewart," she said. "I was very hot working in the fields. I wanted to stay cool and keep my tunic fresh; so, I removed it," explained She-who-sings-sad-songs.

"A white woman does not work in the fields bare breasted, Mary. Your mother would not approve of your behavior. How will I ever explain to your mother, my dearest friend, that I allowed her daughter to become like a heathen. Remember your upbringing Mary. Remember your dear mother, and all that she taught you."

She remembered Ma, all right, and remembered how Ma smelled as she bent over her, teaching her to sew small, even stitches. She remembered Ma's sweet voice as Ma sang her the cradlesongs. But try as she would, she could no longer remember Ma's face. And that made her feel awful.

That evening, Little Squirrel asked She-who-sings-sad-songs what was troubling her. In the Indian language, that she now knew as well as English, She-who-sings-sad-songs tried to make Little Squirrel understand how she felt. "My sister," said She-who-sings-sad-songs, "my heart is torn. I love you and our brother Rain Boy. Our mother Quiet Doe is gentle and kind with me. Our father Netawatwees is wise and patient with me. But I cannot stop thinking about my white family. I have a white brother, whom I love. My white mother is also gentle and kind. My white father is wise and patient.

"My sister, I am lost. I want to belong to a family forever. I cannot find my place. My mind tells me my place is here, where I am happy with you, Little Squirrel. But Angry Woman scolds me and tells me that I betray my white family by my happiness. My sister, I weep with not knowing my place."

Little Squirrel hugged She-who-sings-sad-songs, and kept quiet. When She-who-sings-sad-songs's shoulders stopped shaking from her weeping, Little Squirrel spoke: "My sister, She-who-sings-sad-songs, I want you to find your place here, but I can not make you feel that in your heart if it is not already so. Let us go now and talk to the Grandfather. Perhaps he can help guide you to your true path."

Chapter 6

The Legend of Lost Opportunity

Together, they went to Grandfather's wigwam, and She-who-sings-sad-songs told him of her troubled heart. When she had finished, Grandfather spoke: "Granddaughter She-who-sings-sad-songs, I have watched you as you work in the cornfield across the river. Your music has reached my ears from across the waters of the Cuyahoga. The songs bring great sadness to my heart, Granddaughter. Though I do not understand the words you sing, I know that your heart, as well as your song, is also sad. As I watched and listened to you, I remembered a story told to me by my grandmother. The story is an old Lenni Lenape legend about one such as you. Granddaughter, I will tell you that story now, so that you might find peace within your heart.

"Long before the white men came to this land, there lived a beautiful Lenni Lenape Princess. She was so special that Kitche Manitou, the Creator, wished to bestow upon her the gifts of faith and understanding. So Kitche Manitou led the princess to a cornfield, where the Great Spirit spoke to her, saying, 'Beautiful Princess, you are approaching womanhood. In this cornfield before you are many ears of corn. Those who walk through this cornfield and pluck good ears of corn, with faith and honesty in their hearts, shall be happy and mightily blessed.

Their blessing shall be in proportion to the size and beauty of the ear of corn that they pluck.'"

The Grandfather paused and looked at the two girls who were listening to him--Little Squirrel, the granddaughter of his blood and She-who-sings-sad-songs, the granddaughter of his heart. Then he continued.

"Kitche Manitou told the Princess that she could pass through the cornfield but once, and pluck for herself an ear of corn. She must continue to walk forward, and never take a backward step. The Great Spirit warned her to be careful in her choice of corn, and to pick an ear that was full and fair, that would be good medicine to her for all of her life.

"The Princess offered her thanks to Kitche Manitou and began to move forward through the cornfield. She saw many ears of corn, large, beautiful, good, ripe, sweet. Any one of these would have given her good medicine for her life. But the Princess passed them all by in her eagerness to find the very best of all the ears of corn.

"As the day passed, the Princess came to the far edge of the cornfield where the cornstalks were shorter, and the ears of corn not so good. She remembered all the good ears of corn she had so recently passed by. She then found herself at the end of the cornfield without having plucked an ear of corn. The Princess returned to her village and told her friends not to follow in her footsteps. That night, she disappeared from her village. All she left behind was this story, which the Lenni Lenape call *The Legend of Lost Opportunity.*"

Grandfather looked at She-who-sings-sad-songs and smiled. "Take heed of this story, Granddaughter, or you may find yourself alone and sad for all your days, just like the Lenni Lenape Princess."

"Thank you Grandfather," said She-who-sings-sad-songs. "The Legend speaks to me. Surely I must look within myself for my happiness. Neither my Indian family nor my white family can choose for me a perfect ear of corn. I choose to be useful and good on my own. The Great Spirit has put me on this earth for a purpose, and I will fulfill that purpose and never stray far from the good and honest path."

She-who-sings-sad-songs and Little Squirrel returned to their wigwam, with much to think about.

In the Delaware Indian culture, the women were responsible for planting and tending the crops. This sketch by Edith Steinkraus shows the women and children preparing the soil for planting. (Used with permission.)

Chapter 7

Wampum and Tomahawk

She-who-sings-sad-songs found peace and happiness living with her Indian family. Her life was full of purpose, and she worked hard tending the crops, looking after Rain Boy, and making the clothing that would keep the family warm and dry. Mrs. Stewart continued to scold her, reminding her not to forget her white family in Pennsylvania. Sometimes Mrs. Stewart, in hushed tones, talked to her about "escaping" the Indian village, which made her afraid. She-who-sings-sad-songs didn't want to run away, but she still wished she could see her white family again.

Then one brilliant fall afternoon, something happened that brought back all the horror of the day when she was captured.

She-who-sings-sad-songs and Little Squirrel were gathering roots and nuts on the trail not far from the village. Little Squirrel had wandered off toward the river in search of chestnuts. She-who-sings-sad-songs searched for roots along the trail. She-who-sings-sad-songs was bending down, digging up a root to add to the family's stew pot when she first sensed the danger. The skin on the back of her neck prickled and gooseflesh rose on her arms. She was being watched, she just *knew* it.

Dropping her basket of roots, She-who-sings-sad-songs whirled around, ready to run towards the place she had last seen Little Squirrel. Too late! There, on the trail in front of her, was a party of braves led by the most fearsome Indian she had ever seen, in full war paint. These Indians weren't members of the Turtle Tribe of the Lenni Lenape.

She-who-sings-sad-songs had watched war parties of the Turtle Tribe as they prepared for war. She knew what war paint looked like, and there could be no doubt now--these Indians were painted for war. Then the chief Indian spoke to her. "I seek the village of Chief Netawatwees of the Turtle Tribe. I am Ponti-ac, Chief of the Ottawas. I come in peace. I ask for war."

She-who-sings-sad-songs opened her mouth to call for Little Squirrel, but no sound came out. This Indian was awesome and he frightened her badly. Except for a loin cloth and moccasins, the Indian called Pontiac was naked. He had tattooed bands on his neck, waist, stomach, buttocks, chest, legs, arms and feet. In the center of his chest was tattooed a picture of a glowing sun. Where he was not tattooed, he was painted a bright red, from head to foot. A crescent-shaped stone dangled from his nose, and from his pierced ears hung circlets of bright colored beads. She-who-sings-sad-songs stared at Pontiac and breathed one word, "mother." She said it in English.

Pontiac spoke to one of his braves standing behind him. The young Indian walked to the place where She-who-sings-sad-songs sat trembling and took her arm. Gently, he guided her back to the trail that led to her village. She-who-sings-sad-songs's knees shook, and her hands were like ice. What did these Indians want? Surely the Ottawas would not make war upon the Turtle Tribe of the Lenape. Her father Netawatwees told her that the Indians now only made war upon the British soldiers who stole their land.

She-who-sings-sad-songs looked around for Little Squirrel, but she didn't see her. She-who-sings-sad-songs hoped that her sister was safe. The young brave at her side spoke again, "Come. We go now to the village of the Turtle Tribe. You will come with us."

They arrived at the village. Little Squirrel was waiting for her, and she was calm; she had seen Pontiac and his braves and had run ahead to tell her father. Chief Netawatwees had already assembled his braves around the council fire. The village was filled with tension, for everyone wondered why Pontiac was making this visit to their village.

Pontiac marched proudly to greet Netawatwees at the council fire. "Greetings, Netawatwees, from the Ottawa nation. We come in peace, to ask for war."

Pontiac held up a belt of black wampum and a tomahawk, painted bright red. She-who-sings-sad-songs recognized these as the Indian symbols of war, but war against whom? Little Squirrel joined her and stood quietly at her side. Pontiac continued, "We invite the Turtle Tribe to join us and other tribes from the south and the west to fight against the British who take our hunting grounds.

"One by one, our Indian tribes have been driven out of their homelands--the Chippewa, the Potowatomie, the Wyandot, the Kickapoo, the Miami, the Shawnee, the Fox, and Sauk, the Seneca, the Cayuga and you, the Lenape."

All of the Indians around the fire made sounds of agreement. Netawatwees raised his hand for silence and Pontiac continued speaking. "We cannot fight the mighty British army, each tribe alone. But all tribes together could form one mighty Indian nation. Together, we could fight the British and take back our sacred hunting grounds.

"I ask you to join us, warriors of the Turtle Tribe. Never again must we watch our children and our squaws starve for lack of game. Never again must we watch while our people die from the white man's diseases. I ask you now, brothers of the Turtle Tribe of the Lenni Lenape, join together with our brother tribes to fight against the British."

Pontiac raised the black wampum belt and the red tomahawk high over his head, and many of the Indian braves whooped and cheered. Even some of the women shouted their agreement. She-who-sings-sad-songs's heart sank as she watched her father Netawatwees accept the belt of black wampum and the red tomahawk from Pontiac.

She-who-sings-sad-songs meets Pontiac, great chief of the Ottawa. (Illustration by Judy Botz Newhall.)

Chapter 8

The War Party

She-who-sings-sad-songs willed herself to stay awake, waiting for the dawn. But sometime before the first rays of light were visible through the smoke hole at the top of the wigwam, she fell asleep and slept deeply. Now she awoke with a start, and pushed aside the skin that formed the door of her family's home.

Outside, the warriors were gathering around a red painted post, set into the middle of the clearing. In the red light of dawn, the post looked as if it was covered with blood. The warriors began to chant the traditional song of the Lenape braves going against their enemy:

Oh thou Great Spirit above!
Give me strength and courage
   to meet my enemy,
Suffer me to return again to my children,
To my wife
And to my relations.
Take pity on me and preserve my life
And I will make to thee a sacrifice.

She-who-sings-sad-songs saw Quiet Doe with the other women. They were all busy helping the braves prepare for their journey. And then She-who-sings-sad-songs saw Netawatwees in the group of warriors. He looked fearsome in his war paint. His face was covered with black grease, and across his cheeks were slashes of red paint. Most of the braves had their hair cut short on both sides of their heads, leaving a longer tuft in the center. Netawatwees also wore his hair this way, and he had a braided scalp lock at the back of his head. He kept his hair smooth and black with a mixture of soot and bear fat.

"Little Squirrel, wake up," said She-who-sings-sad-songs to her sister while Rain Boy still slept soundly. "The braves prepare to leave our village. We must say good-bye to our father Netawatwees." The girls left the wigwam and joined the women gathered in the clearing. Netawatwees spoke:

"Lenni Lenape, braves of the Turtle Tribe," he called, "a black cloud hangs over our land. The English Long Knives take from us our lands and our game. No longer can we feed our squaws and our children, and we watch them starve and die in misery. And for our furs, the English Long Knives give us half of what our friends, the French, give us.

"Braves of the Lenape, let us revenge our losses and lift the hatchet against our enemies. Let us strike the painted post and take back that which was stolen from us."

All of the braves formed a circle around the fire and began to chant and dance, brandishing their hatchets and war clubs. Many of the braves had knives and guns they had bought from the French traders who frequently visited their village.

The women stood apart from the braves, chanting, some shaking ceremonial rattles made from the shells of turtles. Just when it seemed to She-who-sings-sad-songs that the commotion would shake down all the wigwams, the braves broke the circle, and still whooping, one by one they struck the painted post with their weapons, showing what they would do to their enemies. Then, on foot, the braves disappeared into the forest. The women continued their chant, beseeching the Great Spirit Manitou to grant victory and keep the braves safe. Little Squirrel chanted with them, but She-who-sings-sad-songs remained silent. She was afraid.

She-who-sings-sad-songs listened to the chanting prayers and shivered in the early morning cold. She pulled her bearskin robe tightly around her shoulders and went to find Grandfather. He always knew how to ease her fears.

Grandfather, like most of the old Lenni Lenape men and women, often entertained the village with his stories of the tribe. His memory was long and clear, and he never varied a story in its telling, no matter how often he repeated it. Grandfather and all of the aged men and women of the village were often sought out by the young, and their advice was cherished. To be granted a conversation by a Grandfather or Grandmother was an honor.

She-who-sings-sad-songs found Grandfather at home in his wigwam. He had not joined the others in sending off the warriors.

"Grandfather," said She-who-sings-sad-songs, "My heart is heavy and I am afraid. I fear that I will not see my father, Netawatwees, or the other braves return from the forest. I fear also for my white family in Pennsylvania, that they might die in this war.

"Grandfather, I am troubled by the many changes we must make, and afraid of that which will come. Please speak words to bring peace and courage to my heart."

She-who-sings-sad-songs then fell silent, carefully watching her Grandfather's face. Not once had he looked at her during her questioning, and he did not look upon her face now. Finally, he spoke:

"Granddaughter, the ground on which you sit was not always the home of the Lenni Lenape wigwam. Once, our people lived in the land where the day begins, near the great salty water. When the white faces came in their winged canoes, our ancestors shared the land and the water with them.

"Granddaughter, in the beginning, the Lenni Lenape and the white faces lived in peace and harmony. But then, many white faces came and cleared the land. For the white faces' gifts, some of our ancestors agreed to trade their homeland to the settlers. When I was a boy, my family left the village of my ancestors to make our home in the hills of Kittatinny.

"Granddaughter, that place was the homeland of your father, Netawatwees. That is where he was born and where he grew for ten seasons. One day, two white men came to our village to show us a piece of paper. The men said they were the sons of William Penn, the white face who honors all Lenni Lenape treaties. The men said that the piece of paper was a treaty that gave them our hunting land.

"Granddaughter, the white faces said that this land went as far from the creek as a man could walk in a day and a half. So that we might determine the boundaries, the sons of Penn invited witnesses to watch a man walk for a day and a half. My son

Netawatwees and I went with others from our tribe to the forest to watch.

"Granddaughter, when we got to the creek, we saw not one walker, but three walkers. The sons of William Penn said they would give a prize to the walker who walked the longest distance. White men on horses carried food and water for the walkers, and they covered a great distance at great haste.

"Your father, Netawatwees, and I could not keep up. The walkers should have walked a few miles, then rested, then shot a squirrel for food in the way of the Lenape. Then the spirit of the treaty would have been honored.

"Granddaughter, in this way, much more of our land was taken from us than was intended. That is how we came to leave our homeland and make our village here. Now the British again seek to take our hunting grounds from us. Our food grows scarce and the Long Knives say that this land belongs to them. The great chiefs, like Pontiac and your father Netawatwees, hope to take back their tribal lands and hunting grounds so that once more we may live in bounty and peace."

When Grandfather stopped speaking, he looked at She-who-sings-sad-songs. She understood better why her father and the other braves had to leave the village. But understanding the past did not calm her fears about the future.

"Grandfather, I thank you for your wise words, but tell me, how can I calm my fear about what is yet to come? I am powerless against the evil spirits of death and hunger and loneliness. It is not for myself I fear, but for those I love--for my Indian family here, and my white family I left behind."

Grandfather looked into her eyes and touched her face with his hand: "Granddaughter, Manitou, the Great Spirit, has given a purpose to all things. Manitou has told the moon to light the earth at night. He has told the rain to water the crops and keep our Mother, the earth, fresh and clean. Manitou has told the winds of the north to bring the snows that help us track the deer. And Granddaughter, Manitou has given to you a purpose. The Great Spirit of Manitou has told you what you must do to find peace in your heart. Go now, Granddaughter, and find your peace."

She-who-sings-sad-songs thanked Grandfather and went to find Little Squirrel. She wanted to share with her sister all that Grandfather had told her.

Chapter 9

Blankets of Death

Before the corn was waist high, Netawatwees and his warriors returned, safely, to the village on the Cuyahoga. Netawatwees told She-who-sings-sad-songs and Little Squirrel that the Indians had made a temporary peace with the soldiers at Fort Pitt. She-who-sings-sad-songs was glad that no scalps were taken on either side.

On the day he returned, Netawatwees presented each of his children with blankets given to him during a truce at Fort Pitt. Little Squirrel's blanket was bright blue, the color of the summer sky. She-who-sings-sad-songs's blanket was woven in a red and blue plaid. Rain Boy's blanket was chestnut colored, with a red edge. Rain Boy was so pleased with his gift that he carried the blanket over his shoulder everywhere he went, even though it was the middle of the summer and very hot. She-who-sings-sad-songs and Little Squirrel hid their smiles, not wanting to embarrass the little boy who, was so proud of his new blanket.

At mid-summer, Netawatwees once again prepared to go to war because three forts still remained in British hands. But before the war party could leave, catastrophe visited the Indian village, effectively removing the Turtle Tribe from the war.

By fall, nearly half of the Turtle Tribe was wiped out by a terrible disease. Mrs. Stewart said it was small pox.

White Eyes, the tribe's *shaman*, or medicine man, said it was an evil spirit. Chief Netawatwees said it was the white man's curse.

Rain Boy was the first to die. It started with the chills. Even though the day was warm, Rain Boy lay all morning in the wigwam, wrapped in his red and brown blanket.

"Rain Boy, what is wrong with you today that you do not want to play in the river with your friends?" asked She-who-sings-sad-songs of the little boy in the blanket.

"I am cold, sister," he replied shivering, though the wigwam was warm.

"I will tell our father, Netawatwees, that you are ill," she said. "Perhaps he will take you to *pimook*; go to sweat. The warmth of the steam will restore you, little brother." She-who-sings-sad-songs selected some roots and herbs from the family's store of medicines and set them to brew in a large kettle of water before she ran off to find Netawatwees.

The people of the village often went to the sweat houses for relief of illnesses or just to relax. The men and the women had separate sweat houses, a short distance away from the main village. Each sweat house was dug into the earth and covered with a wooden roof and dirt. One low door allowed the "sweaters" to creep into the structure and then seal it off.

Netawatwees carried his son to the men's sweat house, and She-who-sings-sad-songs followed, carrying the kettle of herbs and water. Just outside the building, many round stones, each one the size of a turnip, were heating in a smoldering fire. Rain Boy crawled inside the sweat house while his father rolled several of the hot stones in after him. She-who-sings-sad-songs gave her father the kettle, and he, too, crawled into the sweat house, closing the door behind him. When Netawatwees poured the liquid over the hot stones, it created a soothing steam to help Rain Boy get well.

But by nightfall, Rain Boy was burning with fever. The next day, a rash covered his face, hands and feet. She-who-sings-sad-songs, Quiet Doe, and Little Squirrel took turns soothing the little boy as his body fought the disease. But by the fourth day, the disease had spread to others in the village, as well.

On the seventh day, Rain Boy died. She-who-sings-sad-songs thought her heart would break, and even Little Squirrel could not console her. She-who-sings-sad-songs painted her face and her body black, as did the rest of the family and friends of the once happy and lively little boy. She and Little Squirrel helped their mother dress the corpse in new clothes and wrap it in the blanket Rain Boy had so loved.

Then Netawatwees gently placed the body of his little son into a bark coffin made by his own hands. Inside the coffin, Quiet Doe placed all of Rain Boy's favorite toys: his spoon and cup, his knife, and skins for new moccasins. Grandfather cut a hole into the bark of the coffin near Rain Boy's head so that his spirit could come and go as it liked until it found a final resting place. Finally, the coffin was lowered into the earth and covered with dirt.

At dusk, She-who-sings-sad-songs returned to the grave and left a kettle of food for her brother. She vowed to return each evening and leave food until she was sure that Rain Boy had found his final resting place and no longer needed to eat. Never again would anyone in the village speak the name of Rain Boy, for to do so would increase his family's grief.

Although She-who-sings-sad-songs and Quiet Doe continued to grieve for the little boy, they kept very busy tending to Little Squirrel, who was the next to fall ill. She-who-sings-sad-songs prayed for her sister's life. Little Squirrel--her sister and friend-- couldn't die. She-who-sings-sad-songs wouldn't let her.

Gently, She-who-sings-sad-songs bathed Little Squirrel's fevered body with cool water from the river. She helped Quiet Doe prepare a soothing herb broth for Little Squirrel to drink. And when the itching, oozing rash appeared on Little Squirrel's body, it was She-who-sings-sad-songs who applied the soothing ointments.

After many days, Little Squirrel did get better, but her face was covered with scars from the rash. All of the Indians who recovered from the dreadful disease were scarred for life. Mrs. Stewart said that it was God's punishment on the wicked heathen, but She-who-sings-sad-songs knew that was not true. Little Squirrel had never hurt anyone or anything in her whole life.

One night, as She-who-sings-sad-songs was applying ointment to Little Squirrel's rash, she heard Quiet Doe talking to her husband, Netawatwees. Quiet Doe said, "I have heard that this white man's disease has also killed many Shawnee and Mingo. How is it, my husband, that this disease travels so quickly through the villages?"

There was a long silence before She-who-sings-sad-songs heard Netawatwees reply. "Quiet Doe, my wife, three moons ago I traveled to Fort Pitt with warriors from the Shawnee and Mingo nations. After the siege, we made a truce with the British warrior Bouquet. We agreed to no longer attack Fort Pitt. Bouquet is pleased and gives us blankets as a gift to seal the truce.

"My wife, it was I who brought the smallpox to our people, inside the gift blankets."

Quiet Doe did not reply.

Chapter 10

The French Trader

She-who-sings-sad-songs stood outside the family wigwam and stirred the pot of stew thickened with cornmeal. The stew was fragrant with fresh venison and vegetables, seasoned with wild onions. The stew simmered over the fire all day. Whenever anyone was hungry, he would fill his bowl and sit by the fire to eat.

Earlier in the morning, She-who-sings-sad-songs had made bread. First, she pounded the dried grains of ripe corn into the fine flour. Then she added pared chestnuts and a bit of maple sugar for flavor, and slowly added water. For a long time, she sifted and kneaded the mixture into a dough, carefully shaping it into round cakes about six inches in diameter and one inch thick. Finally she placed the corn cakes into the good, clean ashes of an oak bark fire and baked them until they were golden.

It was fall now, and although the days were warm, the nights were getting cooler. She-who-sings-sad-songs, Little Squirrel and Quiet Doe spent most of their autumn days curing meat and fish, and drying and storing nuts, grain and vegetables. The corn, beans and squashes had been harvested, and the storehouses were filled with enough food to feed the village during the winter. Some of the corn was already dry, including the popcorn. The husks were peeled back and braided in bunches, and the corn was hung to dry inside the wigwam. Some of the corn was saved as seed for the next year's crops, and this corn would never be eaten, even if the winter was hard and there was nothing left to eat.

She-who-sings-sad-songs was fifteen summers old now. She had been living with the Indians for so long that she no longer thought of her name as Mary. Only Mrs. Stewart called her by that name. To everyone else, including herself, she was She-who-sings-sad-songs.

The memories of her family in Pennsylvania, however, remained with her. Even though she could no longer see their faces in her mind, certain memories were still vivid. As she stirred the mush, She-who-sings-sad-songs thought about her white family:

She remembered her mother's calm voice, teaching her to sew, telling her to take very small stitches; she remembered her father as he sat at the rough table at the end of the day, hands folded, head bowed, asking God to bless their evening meal; and she remembered her brother Dougal showing her how to milk Bossy, the family cow that supplied them with fresh milk.

In her mind's eye, she could see their shapes, even remember what they were wearing; but try as she would, she could not envision their faces.

Her memories were interrupted by the excited cries of the children playing near the river. "Joo, joo, joo," they yelped, as they splashed in the shallow water. She-who-sings-sad-songs looked to see what made them so excited. A man in buckskins was pulling his canoe up on shore, and the children were gathered around him. He was the French trader, Saguin.

"Father, our friend Saguin pays us a visit," said She-who-sings-sad-songs. Netawatwees had just returned that morning from a hunting trip. Tonight there would be fresh venison to eat with the corn mush. Netawatwees walked to where she stood and together they watched as Saguin delighted the children with gifts. The trader gave them strings of colored beads, little mirrors, combs, and buttons to decorate their clothing. He brought only gifts with him today. Nearly all of Saguin's trading business had already taken place at his trading post on the Cuyahoga, a few miles to the north of the Indian village. At his trading post, Saguin stocked tools, knives, blankets, coats, and metal cooking pots. With these wares, he would bargain for beaver, fox, wildcat, muskrat, mink, deer and bear furs. Saguin never traded guns or ammunition with the Indians, but he knew others who did.

"Our friend travels light," said Netawatwees to She-who-sings-sad-songs, looking at the half empty canoe. They couldn't know that Saguin carried the heaviest burden of all: a message that would forever change both their lives.

Saguin looked up at them and raised his hand in greeting. He took a pouch from his canoe and walked toward She-who-sings-sad-songs and Netawatwees.

"*Bonjour*, my friend, chief of the Turtle Tribe," said Saguin. "I greet you. I bring gifts for you and your family," he said as he held up the pouch. Also, I have news for you, *mon ami*. But first, we eat, no?"

Quiet Doe and Little Squirrel came out of the wigwam at the sound of the trader's voice. Quiet Doe stood beside her husband and spoke:

"Saguin, our friend, you must join us for our evening meal and share our campfire. We welcome you."

That evening, She-who-sings-sad-songs and her family and the French trader feasted on venison stew and the tasty corn cakes baked that morning. They also ate fresh squash from their garden, cooked in maple syrup until the pieces were sweetly glazed. They washed it all down with cool water from the river Cuyahoga.

Saguin brought forth the gifts he had promised. To Netawatwees, he gave a small knife with a carved wooden handle. To Quiet Doe he gave a packet of needles, smooth and sharp. And to Little Squirrel and She-who-sings-sad-songs, he gave scissors--one pair to each girl. Everyone was delighted, and they chatted happily with the trader around the campfire as they sipped an herb tea that Quiet Doe made for them.

When they finished with the tea, Saguin grew very quiet. She-who-sings-sad-songs thought the trader looked very sad, and she wondered what was wrong. She didn't have to wait long.

"Great Chief of the Turtle Tribe," said Saguin. "I bring news of the English leader Bouquet. As we speak, Bouquet and his army await at Newcomers-town on the Tuscarawas to finalize a peace agreement with all the Indian nations."

She-who-sings-sad-songs' heart soared at his piece of news. She looked closely at the face of her father, Netawatwees; his face was expressionless. Then the trader continued:

"Bouquet says that all white captives taken by the Indians must be returned to him at Coshocton before the new moon. Bouquet and his army are prepared to attack any Indian village that refuses to surrender their prisoners."

Little Squirrel, who was sitting beside She-who-sings-sad-songs, reached over and took her sister's hand. "My sister is not a white captive. She-who-sings-sad-songs is an Indian woman now," said Little Squirrel.

Little Squirrel began to cry. She said to Neta-watwees, "Father, please. Don't turn my sister over to the English warrior Bouquet. Her place is here with us."

Netawatwees stared into the fire and was very quiet for a long time. Finally, he spoke. "My daughter She-who-sings-sad-songs must decide for herself if she wishes to stay or to go."

British Colonel Henry Bouquet took part in the peace negotiations that followed Pontiac's Rebellion. In this Benjamin West engraving, Bouquet meets with the Indians in 1764. (Courtesy of Rare Books and Manuscripts Division, The New York Public Library, Astor, Lenox and Tilden Foundation.)

The Indian Trader by Frank Wilcox. Photographed from *Ohio Indian Trails* (Copyright 1970). (Used with permission of the Kent State University Press.)

Chapter 11

The Parting

In the end, there was no choice, She-who-sings-sad-songs knew. If she decided to stay, the white chief Bouquet might sweep down upon the village and kill them all for refusing to obey. So She-who-sings-sad-songs told Netawatwees and Quiet Doe and Little Squirrel that she would go.

On the day of their departure, Mrs. Stewart could barely contain her excitement. Seagull had given her a new bonnet as a parting gift, a bonnet like all proper English women wore. Except for the bonnet, though, Mrs. Stewart was dressed like an Indian woman. Her hair was tied back, Indian fashion, and she wore a deerskin tunic and leggings.

She-who-sings-sad-songs couldn't exactly remember what white women wore or what her own mother would look like. She looked down at her moccasin-clad feet. Would Ma and Pa and Dougal even recognize her? Had she changed that much over the years? She-who-sings-sad-songs worried that she might never find her family and they might never recognize her.

With long and tender embraces, She-who-sings-sad-songs said tearful good-byes first to Quiet Doe, and then to the rest. With tears in her eyes, she made the rounds. Likewise, many of her Indian friends also cried. Netawatwees watched on in silence. She-who-sings-sad-songs had become accustomed to the Indian way of life and he knew she would find it hard to adjust to the world of the white faces. She-who-sings-sad-songs finished her good-byes. Her leaving those she loved might prevent more bloodshed between the two races, and that hope gave her the courage she needed to say farewell. Perhaps one day, the Indians and the white faces could live together in the same world in peace.

They planned the journey as best they could. She-who-sings-sad-songs and Mrs. Stewart would travel to the camp of the English soldiers by canoe, accompanied by Netawatwees and Little Squirrel.

During a moment when Mrs. Stewart was alone with She-who-sings-sand-songs, she became very anxious and wanted to be on the way. "Hurry, Mary. If we leave soon, we could be at Coshocton by tomorrow morning. Think of it, Mary! By tomorrow, we will be in the bosom of our families at last!"

"One moment, Angry Woman," pleaded She-who-sings-sad-songs. She spoke in the Lenape language. For once, Mrs. Stewart didn't scold her for talking like a heathen. "First, I must say good-bye to my Grandfather."

Grandfather was very old now. She-who-sings-sad-songs went to his wigwam and found him sitting inside, waiting for her. The old man reached for her hand, and into her palm he placed three seeds.

"Granddaughter, take these seeds, one from each of the three sisters--the bean, the squash, the corn. Keep these three with you as you journey through the cornfield. Plant them in your heart."

She-who-sings-sad-songs closed her fingers around the three shiny seeds. She could feel the warmth and the life within the tiny kernels. She opened her hand and looked at the seeds. Grandfather pointed to the squash seed and said, "This, Granddaughter, is the seed of the white faces. Like the white faces, the vines of the squash spread over the land."

Then Grandfather pointed to the kernel of corn and said, "This, Granddaughter, is the seed of the Indians. Like the cornstalk, we grow tall and straight."

"And this seed, Granddaughter," he said, pointing to the bean seed, "is you! Remember that you, like the bean plant, needed the support of the cornstalk as you became a woman."

She-who-sings-sad-songs replied, "I shall never forget this lesson, my Grandfather, and I will plant the seeds of your wisdom in my heart for all eternity. Nor will I forget either, Grandfather, that the three sisters-- the squash, the corn, and the bean--always are planted together in the bosom of our mother, the earth, where they will grow and sustain each other until the final harvest."

Without another word, without a tear, She-who-sings-sad-songs left Grandfather's wigwam.

It took most of the morning to portage, or carry, the two canoes from the Cuyahoga River to the Tuscarawas River. Coshocton, where Bouquet's army awaited the return of the white captives, was on the Tuscarawas, a two-day journey south.

The canoes they carried were made from the bark of the elm tree. She-who-sings-sad-songs remembered the time when Netawatwees and Rain Boy worked with the other men of the village to make the sturdy canoes in which they would travel. Her throat ached, but she swallowed her tears as she remembered Rain Boy working cheerfully alongside the bigger men to remove the bark of a giant elm tree. Then the men inserted pine saplings inside the bark to form the ribs of the canoe. The ribs would give the canoe its shape even when the bark dried. The ends of the bark were sewn together at the stern and the bow with fibers from the root of the tamarack. Rain Boy had then sealed the seams and cracks with pine pitch to make the canoe water-tight.

Sometimes, the Lenape made dugout canoes from burned-out tree trunks, but these vessels were heavy and cumbersome to carry for long distances. Canoes made from bark were light enough for the travelers to carry on their shoulders, one person on each end. Now, Netawatwees and Angry Woman carried one of the canoes, and Little Squirrel and She-who-sings-sad-songs carried the other. As they walked the well-worn portage path, She-who-sings-sad-songs and Little Squirrel talked.

"Little Squirrel, my home in Pennsylvania was near the great Fort Pitt. Sometimes, our father Neta-watwees travels to Fort Pitt to council with the white soldiers. Perhaps you could go there with him one time and we could meet," said She-who-sings-sad-songs.

"Yes, perhaps," said Little Squirrel. She smiled at She-who-sings-sad-songs, and kept walking. It was enough to be together now, walking in the warm autumn sunlight through the sweet smelling forest.

By mid-morning, the four travelers reached the Tuscarawas, where they put their canoes into the river. She-who-sings-sad-songs and Little Squirrel went in one canoe and Netawatwees and Mrs. Stewart went in the other. That afternoon, the weather changed suddenly. The wind whipped the falling yellow leaves around the travelers. The leaves settled on the water all around them. By night fall the trees would be bare.

The temperature dropped and it began to rain, so the travelers took shelter for the night, wrapped in blankets from Saguin's trading post, huddled under the overturned canoes. The next morning they made an early start. During the night, the skies had cleared and the wind died down, but now there was an autumn chill in the air even though the sun was shining.

As they approached Coshocton, the banks of the river grew steeper. On the tops of the hills over-looking the river, the travelers could see the camps of Bouquet's army. A stockade had been built close to the river. When the travelers paddled their canoes toward the place where the stockade stood, several soldiers started down the river bank to meet them.

They paddled to the shore and got out of the canoes. (Mrs. Stewart, in her great excitement, nearly overturned the canoe before Netawatwees could maneuver it to shore.) She-who-sings-sad-songs watched as Mrs. Stewart threw herself into the arms of one of the soldiers who had come to the river to accept the surrender of the prisoners.

Then She-who-sings-sad-songs turned to Netawatwees and spoke, her voice choked with sorrow, "You have loved me as a father and I have loved you as a daughter. I will never forget your kindness or your love." Tears streamed down her face. Netawatwees took her face into his great, rough hands and looked deep into her eyes, and he spoke:

"When you were the daughter of my wigwam, your song filled my heart as well as my ears. But from this moment on, you are no longer my daughter. You must go now and sing your songs in the white man's world. Sing happy songs now, Ma-ree." Then the great chief Netawatwees, her father for six years, turned his back on her and would not look at her again.

For the last time, She-who-sings-sad-songs watched as Netawatwees and Little Squirrel paddled their canoes back in the direction from which they had come.

When they were completely out of sight, Mary Campbell turned and walked towards the two soldiers waiting to receive her. Now it was time to find Ma and Pa and Dougal.

The portage to the Tuscarawas. (Illustration by Judy Botz Newhall.)

Chapter 12

The Reunion

The two soldiers approached Mary. The soldiers were the first white men, except for the French trader, that she had seen since she had been living in Netawatwees' village. These men didn't look anything like the bearded, scruffy French trader. They were dressed in brilliant red uniforms and carried bayonets that flashed in the sunshine. Their faces were shaved and their hair was cut short.

One of the soldiers had yellow hair and the bluest eyes Mary had ever seen. Her own eyes were brown, like the Indians. Mary had forgotten that white people could have hair like cornsilk and eyes the color of the summer sky.

Mrs. Stewart was still with the soldier on the river bank. Mary glanced that way now, hoping that the two soldiers coming for her wouldn't separate her from Mrs. Stewart. For once, Mary wanted to be near the woman, especially now that she was afraid. What if she couldn't find Ma and Pa and Dougal? Would she even recognize them? Could she understand them? She was grateful to Mrs. Stewart for making her speak English to her. Although Mary spoke Lenape better, she had never forgotten how to speak English.

Now the two soldiers were in front of her, talking to each other about her as if she wasn't even there.

"This one and the woman over there are Neta-watwees' hostages. Pennsylvania folk. This one was taken as a child--probably will give us a fight. Better tie her hands and hobble her feet so she can't run," the soldier with the blue eyes said.

The other soldier unhooked a coil of rope from his belt and reached for Mary's hands. Mary took a step backwards, and protested in the Lenape language: "No, please. I do not wish to be tied. I come here of my own free will. I will not run away."

The soldier with the rope spat a long stream of brown tobacco juice from the side of his mouth and grinned at Mary. For a moment Mary thought he would leave her alone, but, then, she realized that she had used Lenape instead of English.

"Don't even look like no white girl now," he responded, lunging for her arms and tying her hands together in front of her. "Yer folks'll never recognize ya lookin' more like a squaw than a white girl," he growled as he wound the rope around Mary's wrists.

"Stop that! Just what do you think you are doing, young man! Release this girl at once. We didn't come all through this ordeal to be treated like prisoners by our own folks!" commanded Mrs. Stewart in a stern and resolute voice.

"Just followin' orders, ma'am," said the soldier, tying off the rope.

"I am Abigail Stewart and this girl is Mary Campbell. We have been held captive by the Indians since the spring of 1759, and I for one, will be mighty glad to be back in the bosom of my family. Now untie this girl. She is with me and I will take responsibility until her parents get here."

The soldier with Mrs. Stewart nodded his head, and the soldier with the blue eyes untied Mary's wrists.

"Thank-you," Mary said in English, the words sounding strange to her ears.

"My apology ma'am," said blue eyes to Mrs. Stewart. "Sometimes the ones that have been with the Indians the longest want to stay. COL Bouquet's made a promise to the settlers to see that all the loved ones taken captive get returned to their rightful families. I was just makin' sure this young lady didn't bolt.

"There's many families who traveled here with us from Fort Pitt," the soldier continued. "COL Bouquet expects the heathens to turn over more'n a hundred hostages. We got about fifteen hundred soldiers here waitin' to make sure they do. We'll ride in and get 'em back by force if the Indians refuse to turn 'em over.

"You ladies follow us now," he said. "We'll take you to the captives' tent. If your families are here, that's where they'll be lookin' to find ya."

Mary and Mrs. Stewart followed the soldiers. She wished she could go back to the river and wash off some of the grime of her traveling. She wished she could wash her hair and make fresh braids so that she would look good for her family. Mary glanced over at Mrs. Stewart. Mrs. Stewart had never worn her auburn hair in braids the whole time they lived with the Indians. Mrs. Stewart always fastened her hair into a knot at the nape of her neck. When she lost all of her hair pins, she fastened the hair in place with a smooth stick or a piece of bone.

Mrs. Stewart always wore long sleeves to keep the sun from turning her skin brown. Even in the summer, Mrs. Stewart wore long sleeves and a bonnet when she worked in the cornfield. Her skin was pale, the color of the moon on a clear night, but rough from the hard work.

Mary looked at her own hands and arms, brown from working and playing in the warm sunshine. Why her skin was almost as dark as Little Squirrel's skin by the end of the summer. Only in the winter was Mary's skin pale like Mrs. Stewart's.

Something that the soldier said troubled Mary. He said her family wouldn't recognize her because she looked like a squaw. But Mary wasn't sure she would recognize her white family either. She tried hard, but she could not see their faces in her memory. Mrs. Stewart would remember them, though, thought Mary. That made her feel a little better. I must stay close to Mrs. Stewart so that Ma and Pa and Dougal can find me, she thought.

The soldiers led Mary and Mrs. Stewart to a large clearing surrounded by canvas tents. "This one you can share," said one of the soldiers, until your family gets here. They'll come here eventually to find you if they're here. Those that don't have family comin', we take with us back to Fort Pitt next month."

Inside the tent were two canvas and pole platforms. Mary asked Mrs. Stewart what they were for. Mrs. Stewart said they were called cots, used for sleeping off the ground. On each cot was a bright, woven blanket. The blankets reminded her of the blankets her father Netawatwees had given to her and Little Squirrel and Rain Boy. Mary wondered if these blankets were infected with the white man's disease.

Well, she would take her chances with the blanket, Mary thought, but she could not sleep on that thing called a cot.

That evening, the soldiers came back and brought them something to eat, a stew that Mrs. Stewart said was baked beans. Although Mary was very hungry, she was hesitant to try the dish.

"Why Mary," said Mrs. Stewart, "your Ma made the best baked beans I ever tasted. Baked beans was always your favorite supper when we were in Pennsylvania."

But Mary thought the dish was much too sweet, and she longed for some cornmeal and venison so she could prepare a decent meal.

Mary was day-dreaming about how wonderful a hot venison stew would taste, when she heard Mrs. Stewart scream.

"Joe! Joe Stewart!" Mrs. Stewart was standing beside their campfire, her plate of baked beans spilled at her feet.

Mary saw tears in Mrs. Stewart's eyes. Mary hadn't seen Mrs. Stewart cry since the day Sammy was killed. What was the matter with the woman, thought Mary, and she looked across the clearing to see what Mrs. Stewart was staring at. A man was walking toward them. At first Mary thought he was the French trader. The man was wearing buckskins and on his feet he wore moccasins. He had a full beard and wore his hair long to his shoulders.

"Abby? Abby, love," he exclaimed, and rushed toward Mrs. Stewart. Mrs. Stewart ran to him and they embraced. Mary tried to remember what Mr. Stewart looked like, but she couldn't find this man's face anywhere in her memory.

"Abby, I've never stopped looking for you. I swore in the name of God that I would never rest until I'd saved you from those red savages", said Mr. Stewart to his wife. Mrs. Stewart smiled through her tears and kissed both his hands and then his face. Tears streamed from her eyes.

"I've prayed for this day, Joe. I missed you so much. Thank you for coming."

Then Mrs. Stewart remembered Mary, who was still sitting by the fire with her plate of baked beans.

"This is young Mary--Mary Campbell--did you travel here with her folks?"

Mr. Stewart nodded his head at Mary in greeting. He looked at her closely and then said to his wife:

"I wouldn't have recognized her, Abby, if you hadn't told me her name." Mary was disappointed. Mr. Stewart continued: "After you were taken, I left Pennsylvania to look for you. I never saw the Campbells again. I've settled on a piece of land near Fort Detroit now. Built us a mighty fine cabin. They say Fort Detroit is the strongest fort in these parts--living near it, we'll never again have to fear for Indians."

"Amen," said Mrs. Stewart.

"A party of men is leaving for Fort Detroit first thing tomorrow," her husband continued. "I say, we travel with them. We'll be safer than if we travel alone."

Mary felt sick. Mrs. Stewart looked so happy, but Mary couldn't feel happy for her. If Mrs. Stewart left now, Mary might never find Ma and Pa and Dougal on her own. How would they recognize her? Mr. Stewart hadn't recognized her. But Mrs. Stewart must look the same as she looked when she lived in

Pennsylvania. If Mrs. Stewart stayed with Mary, then her family would be able to find her.

Mary stood up and went to Mrs. Stewart. The woman embraced her. Never in the whole time they lived with the Indians had Mrs. Stewart hugged Mary.

"Mary, child, I hope your Ma thinks I've done right by her wishes for you. I've tried to keep your family's memory alive, but it hasn't always been easy. I hated the red heathens. They killed my baby. Someday, you'll understand," said Mrs. Stewart. "I'll leave you now--I'm done waiting. The good Lord has answered my prayers. Give my best to your family, and tell your Ma how hard I tried with ya," Mrs. Stewart said, and kissed Mary's cheek.

That night after the Stewarts left, Mary took one of the blankets and spread it outside the tent under the stars. She longed for the friendly comfort of Little Squirrel's company and she missed the security of Netawatwees' and Quiet Doe's wigwam. Inside her tunic was a leather bag with the three seeds Grandfather had given her as a parting gift. She clutched the bag to her breast, remembering, and her tears soaked the white man's blanket. She was afraid, and, for the first time in her young life, Mary was truly alone.

Colonel Henry Bouquet and his army camped on the hillside above the Tuscarawas River during the peace negotiations with the Indians in 1764. Today, a marker designates the spot along Ohio route 77. (Photo by Jane Ann Turzillo.)

The Tuscarawas River. Mary Campbell must have canoed over this very stretch of the river as she made her way to COL Bouquet's camp in 1764. (Photo by Jane Ann Turzillo.)

Chapter 13

Song of Freedom

Each day, COL Bouquet received the newly returned captives at the place of council, a rustic arbor of saplings and tree boughs, large enough to shelter the English officers and the Indian chiefs with their hostages. Bouquet's troops were camped on the surrounding hillsides. The troops, nearly 1,500 men, assembled in formation. It was an awesome spectacle.

The soldiers' bayonets flashed in the sun, and the brilliant tartans of the Highland regulars fluttered in the breezes that blew off the Tuscarawas below. The Royal American troops, in their bright red uniforms, stood in long lines--so long that Mary could not see where they ended. In the meadow below the place of council stood the Pennsylvania troops, clad in drab brown uniforms; next to them, bands of Virginia backwoodsmen in fringed hunting clothes and Indian moccasins leaned carelessly on their rifles. If Mary ever had a thought of running back to her Indian family, the spectacle before her put an end to it. Surely, Netawatwees' village stood no chance against these troops.

Anxious families had traveled long distances in the hopes of finding their lost loved ones. These families camped close to the place of council, hoping to get near enough to see each captive turned over to

Bouquet. Most of the captives, Mary noticed, were women and children, but there were a few young men as well. The captives were brought to the clearing where Mary waited, and some were assigned tents until their families arrived at COL Bouquet's camp. Other returned captives were immediately claimed by their excited families.

Mary watched the scenes of joy and of sorrow unfolding before her. One young husband and wife searched for young sons amongst the returned captives. The boys spotted their parents first, and they raced into their waiting arms, happy to see them. Other scenes were not so happy. Several hopeful relatives left in grief, after being told that their loved ones had been killed or had died from disease while in captivity. Some of the returned captives resisted the soldiers and their white families. One young woman was securely tied to her horse before she left COL Bouquet's camp with her family. In the Shawnee language, the woman cursed her family, spat at them, and swore she would return to her Indian husband and baby. But surely the saddest people at the camp were the unclaimed captives, those people, like Mary, who waited and watched for their loved ones to recognize them.

Mary searched every face in the camp for Ma and Pa and Dougal. She studied every feature, hoping to remember something that would link her to one of the hopeful relatives who came to the clearing. But as the days passed, Mary despaired of ever seeing her family again.

Mary closed her eyes and took stock of her memories. She remembered the sweat-and-earth smell of Pa after he came back from clearing the land,

and how glad she was to see him at the end of the long day. But she could not see his face. She remembered the warmth of Dougal's large hands covering her own as he taught her how to milk Bossy in the cold barn. She could almost feel his breath steaming down on the back of her neck as he sat behind her on the three-legged milk stool. In her mind's eye, Mary turned around to look at Dougal, but she could not see his face.

Mary remembered the sweet strains of the cradlesongs her mother hummed to the family each night, after they were all tucked snugly under the quilts. The songs had remained with her all the time she was with her Indian family, but in her memory, it was Ma's voice she heard humming, not her own.

Clearly, sweetly, the music of the lullaby washed over her. It was almost as if Ma was there in the clearing with her. And suddenly, Mary did remember Ma's face, her bright eyes, and how the wisps of her curly hair always framed her face even when she wore a bonnet.

Mary opened her eyes and saw Ma's beautiful face and heard her soothing voice. Mary's knees shook as she took a tiny step toward the beautiful woman who stood before her, humming the haunting tune of her childhood.

"Ma? Ma, it's me, Mary," she said to the beautiful woman. Beside the woman stood a young man. Surely, this must be her brother, Dougal, grown up and bearded. "Dougal Campbell?" she said to him.

Recognition flashed in the woman's eyes, and she held out her arms to Mary. Ma held her tightly, still humming the sweet cradlesong that had brought them together.

Ma and Dougal and Mary sat up late into the night, talking and remembering. Ma told Mary that Pa had wanted to come with her and Dougal to find Mary, but he had to stay behind to take in the harvest. At home with Pa were two of Mary's brothers, born while she was away. Mary was glad that she would be going home to a large family and that she would have plenty to do. Still, Mary thought that a dozen brothers could never take the place of Little Squirrel.

Mary told her mother and brother that she loved them and that she had never forgotten them in her heart. Mary also told them something of her life with her Indian family, but she was careful because she sensed that this talk made them uncomfortable. Whenever she talked about the Indians, her brother Dougal became very angry.

To help her brother understand her feelings, Mary showed Dougal the *three sisters* seeds she had received as a parting gift from Grandfather.

"These three seeds should be planted together in the same field if any of the plants is to grow strong," explained Mary.

Taking her brother's hand, she placed the squash seed into Dougal's open palm and said, "This squash is like my white family. The vines of the squash spread over the ground to hold in the moisture that nourishes all the plants and gives them a strong start."

Then, putting the kernel of corn into Dougal's palm, she added, "This seed of the corn is like my Indian family. This kernel of corn will grow into a strong, tall cornstalk to support the bean plant as she grows."

Mary was about to place the bean seed into Dougal's hand when suddenly he threw the kernel of corn into the campfire.

"Strong and tall, ha, what a story you tell, Mary," Dougal retorted angrily. "Those murderous, thieving Indians won't be planting anywhere--they'll be driven from this land like leaves in the wind. You'll never again have to fear for your safety, Mary. You're back with your family now. Your ordeal is finished, dear sister. It is over."

Mary sighed and leaned against her mother. "Yes," she whispered, "it is over, and it is beginning," Mary said, holding the bean seed tightly in her hand.

Colonel Bouquet's Exchange of Prisoners by Frank Wilcox. Photographed from *Ohio Indian Trails* (Copyright 1970). (Used with permission of the Kent State University Press.)

Epilogue

After her return to her home in Cumberland County, Pennsylvania, Mary married Joseph Willford. They had many, perhaps as many as a dozen children. Mary died in 1801.

Today, descendants of Mary Campbell periodically hold family reunions at the cave on the Cuyahoga River in Ohio where Mary lived with the Indian women and children while the village was being built on the ridge above. In 1934, a monument was erected at that site that names Mary Campbell as "the first white child on the Western Reserve" of Ohio.

After Mary was returned to her white family, the Delaware Indians (Lenni Lenape) continued their gradual migration west. By the year 1817, the Western Reserve of Ohio knew no more the tread of the Indians of the forest. One by one, the land deeds granted to them were taken back, and the Delawares became homeless wanderers, always marching toward the setting sun. During the nineteenth century, the Delaware Nation dwindled from ten thousand to about one thousand souls.

Some of the Delawares eventually settled in Oklahoma, where they joined the Cherokees. Others went up to Canada and joined a Moravian missionary settlement. Some Delawares found employment as guides and scouts for the government or with migrating fur traders. Today, although many Indians are proud of their Delaware ancestors, it is believed that there are few, if any, full-blooded Delaware Indians left in the United States today.

It is a sad footnote to the story of Mary Campbell that her hope of the Indians and white settlers living together supportively--like the three sisters--never came to pass.

Mary Campbell's cave as it looks today. Each year, thousands of visitors hike over the trail that passes by the cave. The area is known as Gorge Park and is maintained by the Akron Metropolitan Park system. (Photo by Jane Ann Turzillo.)

How much of this book is true?

The first account of the Mary Campbell story was recorded by Perrin in his book, "Summit County History," published in 1881. Later versions of the legend appear in an assortment of Ohio history books. The accounts are similar, but details vary. My story follows as closely as possible the research presented in a report from Mrs. J.B. McPherson to the Cuyahoga Falls Chapter of the Daughters of the American Revolution, June 1934.

Although *Song of Courage, Song of Freedom* is a work of fiction, most of the characters in this book are based upon real people. Mary Campbell and Mrs. Stewart were certainly real. At least one history reports that a Sammy Stewart was killed by the Indians as they escaped with the two female captives.

The Indian uprising led by Pontiac is well known. At first, Pontiac was successful in conquering the British forces. But later, when the French refused to help him and other allies deserted him, Pontiac signed a peace agreement and returned to his village on the Maumee River in Ohio. Pontiac was murdered by another Indian who was paid by a British trader to kill him.

The sad story of the smallpox epidemic is also based on fact. During the Indian's siege on Fort Pitt, the refugees living there were suffering from the disease. The commander in chief of the British forces wrote to COL Bouquet, suggesting that Bouquet distribute to the Indians blankets from the smallpox ward, to try to eradicate the entire Indian race.

Bouquet apparently consented, and later a smallpox epidemic spread among the Shawnee, the Mingo and the Delaware Indians. Whether or not the epidemic spread to Netawatwees' village, however, is not certain.

The French trader Saguin had a trading post on the Cuyahoga as early as 1755. He was known to be a friend of the Indians of the area. Saguin once wrote that he did not like and would not trade in guns or ammunition with the Indians, although they brought him furs for other wares.

According to Mary Campbell's descendants, Dougal Campbell was present when his sister was turned over to COL Bouquet, but it is not known for certain whether or not Mary's mother was present. The story of Mary's mother recognizing her from the cradlesong is recorded in several history books, but Campbell descendants told me that it was Dougal who first recognized his sister when Netawatwees surrendered her to Bouquet.

Chief Netawatwees returned his white captives, but he refused to discuss peace terms with COL Bouquet, who deposed the chief and ordered the Delawares to name an alternate chief. Records show that Netawatwees visited Fort Pitt in May of 1765, but it is doubtful that he saw Mary at that time or ever again. Netawatwees and his tribe later founded a village at Newcomerstown, which for a time was the capital of the Delaware Nation.

Today, a bronze plaque at the entrance to the cave commemorates the story of Mary Campbell. (Photo by Jane Ann Turzillo.)

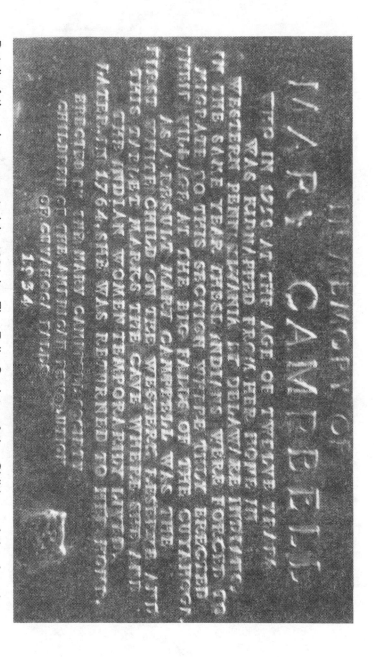

Detail of the plaque erected in 1934 by The Falls Society of the Children of the American Revolution of Cuyahoga Falls. Although this plaque says that Mary was captured at the age of twelve, other sources say she may have been as young as seven years old. In our story, Mary is ten at the time of her capture. (Photo by Jane ann Turzillo.)

INDEX